GOD ALWAYS KEEPS His Promises

TIM LaHAYE
JERRY B. JENKINS

HARVEST HOUSE™ PUBLISHERS

EUGENE, OREGON

Unless otherwise indicated, Scripture verses are from The Holy Bible, King James Version. Verses marked NKJV are taken from the New King James Version. Copyright ©1982 by Thomas Nelson, Inc. Used by permission. All rights reserved. Verses marked NIV are taken from the Holy Bible: New International Version®. NIV®. Copyright © 1973, 1978, 1984 by the International Bible Society. Used by permission of Zondervan Publishing House. The "NIV" and "New International Version" trademarks are registered in the United States Patent and Trademark Office by International Bible Society. Verses marked NASB are taken from the New American Standard Bible®, © 1960, 1962, 1963, 1968, 1971, 1972, 1973, 1975, 1977, 1995 by The Lockman Foundation. Used by permission. (www.Lockman.org)

Some text has been adapted from *Perhaps Today*, copyright © 2001 by Tim LaHaye and Jerry B. Jenkins. Used by permission of Tyndale House Publishers.

"The Empty Cross" previously appeared in *What the Cross Means to Me,* copyright © 2002 by Harvest House Publishers. Used by permission.

Cover by Koechel Peterson & Associates, Inc., Minneapolis, Minnesota

Published in association with Z Strategies, Inc., San Diego, CA.

GOD ALWAYS KEEPS HIS PROMISES
Copyright © 2003 by Tim LaHaye and Jerry B. Jenkins
Published by Harvest House Publishers
Eugene, Oregon 97402
www.harvesthousepublishers.com

Library of Congress Cataloging-in-Publication Data
LaHaye, Tim F.
  God always keeps His promises / Tim LaHaye and Jerry B. Jenkins.
    p. cm.
  ISBN 0-7369-1243-6 (hardcover : alk. paper)
  1. Messiah—Prophecies. 2. Jesus Christ—Messiahship. 3. God—Promises. I. Jenkins, Jerry B. II. Title.
  BT235.L34 2003
  236—dc21   2003002358

Printed in the United States of America.

03 04 05 06 07 08 09 10 11 / RDS-KB / 10 9 8 7 6 5 4 3 2 1

Great Promises
from a Great God

Do you have any idea how many promises there are in the Bible? And do you know how many of them relate directly to you?

While Bible scholars vary on the exact number of promises, at minimum we know there are several hundred! And you would probably be surprised at just how many of them are directed to you and me. These promises show that God cares about us. These assurances are designed to help us face the future with greater courage, to give our lives greater meaning, and to comfort us in the midst of trials. They are given to us to provide strength when we're vulnerable or tempted, to remind us we're never alone, and to speak of the great future God has in store for us.

In the Bible, there's a special set of promises that rises above all the others—promises that relate to the first and second comings of the Lord Jesus Christ. Many of these promises are actually Bible prophecies. At first glance they may seem nothing more than utterances about what will happen in the future. But they also include incredible truths meant to enrich our lives. In this book we'll look at the first-coming prophecies—and promises—and discover the powerful relevance they have to us.

Above all, we'll see that God *always* keeps His promises. People and circumstances may fail you, but not God. Great is His faithfulness to us!

Tim LaHaye

Jerry Jenkins

Contents

*I will put enmity between thee
and the woman, and between
thy seed and her seed; it
shall bruise thy head, and thou
shalt bruise his heel.*

GENESIS 3:15

*When the fulness of the time was
come, God sent forth his Son,
made of a woman...*

GALATIANS 4:4

In the Beginning,
God Made a Promise

God's promises are like the stars; the darker
the night, the brighter they shine.

DAVID NICHOLAS

It seems so ironic that one of the darkest moments in all of history took place in the middle of the only true paradise mankind has ever known—the Garden of Eden.

Can you imagine the brilliance and sparkle of God's new creation? The sky was bluer than blue, the plants were lusher than lush, and all the animals looked glorious in the colorful array in which God coated them. All was perfect. There was nothing more Adam and Eve could ask for. The Bible tells us that every good and perfect gift comes from God, and nothing could have been more good or more perfect than the new creation God gave to Adam and Eve as their home.

But then came along the serpent, and...you know the story. The serpent tempted Adam and Eve to doubt God. God had warned them not to touch the fruit of a certain tree, and the serpent cast doubt upon that warning. God promised a dire consequence, yet the serpent cast doubt upon that promise. Adam and Eve ate the fruit, and the results were instantaneous. "The eyes of them both were opened" (Genesis 3:7). They now had a knowledge of evil. And the rest of Genesis chapter 3 details for us the swift and severe judgment of God upon Adam and Eve's disobedience.

That day, darkness fell upon the Garden. Perfection was no more. Sin had entered the world, bringing with it a horrible separation between people and God. The Lord could no longer fellowship with His creation. With sin came both spiritual and physical death. Spiritual and physical condemnation. Eternal separation from God.

It doesn't get any worse than that, does it? Imagine the great disappointment in God's heart. The heavenly host—God's angels—must have fallen silent in grief. The joy of creation had been replaced with an oppressive sadness and despair.

And it was at that very time—in the darkest of darkness—that God shone the light of His great mercy and grace and gave Adam and Eve hope that not all was lost. It was in this very setting that God proclaimed a wonderful promise.

I will put enmity between thee and the woman, and between thy seed and her seed; it shall bruise thy head, and thou shalt bruise his heel (Genesis 3:15).

What was God saying? That although Satan has already wounded mankind by bruising his heel, there will come one day an individual who will crush Satan's head. The struggle between Satan and the woman's seed will ultimately result in victory for God and those who follow Him. Through Mary, the very human mother of Jesus, God miraculously "sent forth his Son, made of a woman" (Galatians 4:4).

So right from the very beginning —as soon as sin entered our world —God announced

> There is a living God; He has spoken in the Bible. He means what He says and will do all He has promised.
>
> HUDSON TAYLOR

the promise of a Savior for all people. He was not caught off guard; He didn't have to grope around desperately and figure out how to get fallen mankind out of this predicament. God was fully ready with a promise of complete redemption and deliverance.

Yes, the day that sin entered the world was dark indeed. But God responded with a promise that pierced the darkness with a light that would grow brighter and brighter up to the day of Christ's birth. Though the darkness was intense, God's light was more intense. And that light shone at full intensity when the angels appeared to the shepherds that first Christmas day to proclaim the glorious birth of the Lord Jesus Christ. So thrilled were the angels that they could not withhold their excitement: "Glory to God in the highest, and on earth peace, good will toward men" (Luke 2:14).

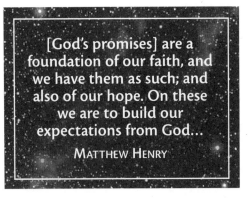

[God's promises] are a foundation of our faith, and we have them as such; and also of our hope. On these we are to build our expectations from God...

MATTHEW HENRY

Though thousands of years had passed, God kept the promise He had made to Adam and Eve. Nothing changed His mind, nothing deterred His plan. In the beginning, God made a promise...and thousands of years later, He fulfilled it. In fact, when Christ was born, many of God's promises came to fruition. You and I, my friend, are the children of a God who always keeps His promises. We can be certain He will keep every one of them. And in the pages to come, we'll discover just how wonderful some of those promises are.

Thine house and thy kingdom shall be established for ever before thee: thy throne shall be established for ever.

2 SAMUEL 7:16

He shall be great, and shall be called the Son of the Highest: and the Lord God shall give unto him the throne of his father David: and he shall reign over the house of Jacob for ever; and of his kingdom there shall be no end.

LUKE 1:32-33

A Forever King with a Forever Kingdom

Eternity to the godly is a day that has no sunset...

If there is one truth we can learn from history, it is this: No king or kingdom lasts forever. The halls of time are littered with the crumbling debris of kingdoms that were once mighty but have fallen. And every human king, no matter how powerful or mighty, has ultimately proven to be a mere mortal. None have defied death. The ancient emperors of Rome, China, and other empires, all of whom built massive dynasties across faraway lands, have long been silenced. The Westminster Abbey in London has witnessed the crowning of 22 monarchs through the past five centuries. How many still wield their scepters today? At one time people said the sun never set on the British Empire, but that's no longer true.

Yet there is one King whose kingdom God has promised will stand forever—King Jesus. And what's especially remarkable is Satan's response to this promise. He has made numerous attempts to prevent Jesus from ever claiming His throne. You may be surprised to know some of those attempts took place long before Jesus ever came to earth.

A thousand years before Jesus was born, God promised King David that the Messiah would come through his family line. God told David, "Thine house and thy kingdom shall be established for ever before thee: thy throne shall be established for ever" (2 Samuel 7:16). In the Psalms, the Lord said to David, "I have made a covenant with my chosen, I have sworn unto David my servant, 'thy seed will I establish for ever, and build up thy throne to all generations'" (89:3-4). In other words, there is a king coming after David whose rule would last for all eternity.

Satan knew that once David's kingdom was established, he was a defeated foe. That's why, through the ages, he tried to prevent God's promise from being fulfilled. Remember the times when the angry King Saul attempted to take David's life? Satan knew that if he could get David out of the picture, the Messiah's family line would come to an abrupt end.

Satan again had his hopes raised when the northern kingdom of Israel was taken into captivity by Assyria and the southern kingdom by Babylon. Perhaps this would bring an end to the kingly line. But no, God kept His promise to bring His people back from Babylon at the end of the captivity. A remnant of the Jewish people returned to Jerusalem and, in time, they rebuilt the Temple and the city walls. The Jewish nation continued onward.

A few hundred years later, when the wise men came from the East to worship little Jesus, King Herod, an evil man, said, "Go and search diligently for the young child; and when ye have found

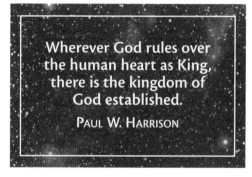

Wherever God rules over the human heart as King, there is the kingdom of God established.

PAUL W. HARRISON

him, bring me word again, that I may come and worship him also" (Matthew 2:8). But worship was far from Herod's mind. Herod was jealous because the wise men had said they were looking for "he that is born King of the Jews." The Roman government had given Herod rulership over the Jewish people, and

Herod wasn't about to relinquish his authority to another. He was afraid Jesus might usurp his throne, and he wanted this challenger killed.

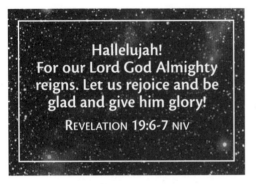

> **Hallelujah!
> For our Lord God Almighty
> reigns. Let us rejoice and be
> glad and give him glory!**
> REVELATION 19:6-7 NIV

That's why, when the wise men failed to reveal where Jesus was, Herod commanded that all the little boys in Bethlehem be slaughtered. Satan inspired this horror in yet another attempt to keep Jesus from claiming His throne.

Satan's fiercest attack came at the cross. Jesus died the most excruciating death imaginable. But not even death could keep Him in the ground. As the apostle Paul said so eloquently, "Death is swallowed up in victory. O death, where is thy sting? O grave, where is thy victory?" (1 Corinthians 15:54-55).

Though Jesus' kingdom has not come yet, His victory is already 100-percent certain. He has already won the battle. And those of us who have received Jesus as Savior can know that our side has already won.

Through the ages, *nothing* has prevented Jesus from one day taking the throne on which David sat.

Even the most powerful spiritual enemy—Satan— has failed in this quest. We who are believers can be fully confident that one day we will live in a forever kingdom ruled by a forever King. It's going to be a perfect kingdom ruled by peace and harmony and righteousness. Never again will we have to fear pain or discouragement. Never again will we suffer or live in trepidation of death. Our King *will* come, and He *will* reign.

Thou, Bethlehem Ephratah,
though thou be little among the
thousands of Judah, yet out of
thee shall he come forth unto me
that is to be ruler in Israel;
whose goings forth have been
from of old, from everlasting.

MICAH 5:2

Now when Jesus was born in
Bethlehem of Judea...

MATTHEW 2:1

The Right Place at
the Right Time

O little town of Bethlehem,
how still we see thee lie!
Above thy deep and dreamless sleep
the silent stars go by;
Yet in thy dark streets shineth
the everlasting Light;
The hopes and fears of all the years
are met in thee tonight.

PHILLIPS BROOKS

an you predict who will be the president of the
United States 100 years from now? How about 500
years from now—that is, if the United States is still
around? And what about going so far as to predict
the very town in which that future president will be
born?

That's an exercise in futility, isn't it? There is simply no way we can know who will serve as the president 100 or 500 years from now or where he or she

will be born. But in a very real sense, that's exactly what one of God's prophets did some 700 years before Jesus Christ was born. The prophet Micah proclaimed, "But thou, Bethlehem Ephratah, though thou be little among the thousands of Judah, yet out of thee shall he come forth unto me that is to be ruler in Israel; whose goings forth have been from of old, from everlasting." Sure enough, Jesus was born in Bethlehem—and the details surrounding the fulfillment of this prophecy are quite remarkable. Whenever I think of this prophecy, I marvel at how God is able to orchestrate a myriad of people and circumstances to fulfill His prophecies down to the very letter—even though many of the participants aren't even aware of what's happening!

Consider, for example, Joseph and Mary. At the time they traveled to Bethlehem, Mary was in the advanced stages of her pregnancy. Scripture tells us she was "great with child" (Luke 2:5). Though she was very near to giving birth, she still climbed on a donkey and made the rough 90-mile journey from Nazareth to Bethlehem. Can you imagine Mary, being "great with child," traveling 90 miles on a donkey? That baby could have been born some other place along the journey. But He wasn't. God planned for the Messiah to be born in Bethlehem.

Now, what spurred Joseph and Mary to go to Bethlehem? At this critical point in Mary's pregnancy, they should have stayed home in the comfortable and familiar surroundings of Nazareth. But it was at this time a Roman ruler commanded that all people return to their city of ancestry

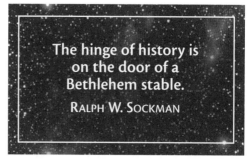

The hinge of history is on the door of a Bethlehem stable.

RALPH W. SOCKMAN

to register for a census (Luke 2:1-3). Bethlehem was Joseph's ancestral home through the lineage of David, and that's where Joseph had to go. No doubt it was God who inspired the Roman ruler with the idea to take a census in order to bring Joseph and Mary to Bethlehem. There was no secret, behind-the-scenes collaborator who conspired to make all this happen just to make sure Micah's prophecy was fulfilled. The census was a massive undertaking that affected people everywhere, and the Romans and the people of Israel were very much at odds with one another. Joseph was obeying a government edict and took his family to Bethlehem, where the Christ child was born—just as God said He would be.

Consider too the precision of Micah's prophecy. He didn't just say the Messiah would be born in Bethlehem, but in "Bethlehem *Ephratah*." You see, there were two Bethlehems at the time of Jesus' birth—one just seven miles to the northwest of Nazareth and the other, Bethlehem Ephratah, to the south near Jerusalem. God wanted to be sure the place of Christ's birth couldn't be confused with any other towns with similar names.

What's more, Micah was precise. He didn't just give a general location in his prophecy. He could have stated that Messiah would be born in the *vicinity* of Jerusalem, for Bethlehem and Jerusalem are only five miles apart. But no—Micah was specific, pinpointing Bethlehem Ephratah as the place of birth.

The LORD is faithful to all his promises, and loving toward all he has made.

PSALM 145:13 NIV

When it comes to fulfilling prophecy, God is exact. That's how it was for *every single one* of the 129 prophecies related to Christ's first coming. And if that's how God worked in relation to Christ's first coming, we can rest assured He will do the very same in connection with the Lord's second coming!

We have no reason to let doubts begin to creep into our minds and cause us to wonder if Christ really is going to return and usher us into His perfect kingdom. God's track record for fulfilling prophecies has always been perfect, and always will be!

Behold, a virgin shall conceive,
and bear a son...
Isaiah 7:14

Now the birth of Jesus Christ
was on this wise: When as
his mother Mary was espoused
to Joseph, before they came
together, she was found with
child of the Holy Ghost.
Matthew 1:18

The God of the Impossible

When God is about to do something great,
He starts with a difficulty. When He is about
to do something truly magnificent,
He starts with an impossibility.

ARMIN GESSWEIN

hrough the ages, people have attempted to explain away the virgin birth. "It's downright impossible for that to happen," they say. And certainly the people who knew Mary and Joseph must have had their doubts. After all, Mary had become pregnant *before* the couple's wedding day. In everyone else's minds, that meant only one thing. If there had been gossip tabloids in those days, this news would have landed her on the front page with extra-bold headlines.

But the fact that Mary was still a *virgin*—even though she was with child—is abundantly clear. In just 13 verses in Luke chapter 1, we read no less than three times that she was a virgin. Matthew tells us,

"Behold, a virgin shall be with child" (1:23). The original Greek word for virgin, *parthenos,* tells us she was pure and chaste and had never known any sexual relations. Also, Matthew was quoting from Isaiah's prophecy about Jesus' birth, where we find the Hebrew word *almah* used to speak of a virgin. This Hebrew term is the most accurate and precise term for virgin used in the Old Testament.

So, God had brought about nothing less than a true miracle in Mary's womb. This wasn't some challenging feat of science. This wasn't some mystical conception of the sort we hear about in ancient mythology. This wasn't some freak of nature. This was the God of the impossible at work. There is only one recorded instance of a virgin ever giving birth to a baby—Mary's birth of Jesus.

> What was true of the Virgin Mary in the history of the Son of God's birth on earth is true of every saint. God's Son is born into me through the direct act of God.
>
> OSWALD CHAMBERS

It would have been totally impossible for any man or woman to fake the fulfillment of this prophecy. Only one woman in all of history can claim that she gave birth to the Messiah. We can know with certainty that Jesus Christ really is the Messiah, for the Bible said He would be born of a virgin, and there is only *one* virgin who has ever given birth to a child.

So the next time you read or sing about the virgin birth, remember just how special an event this was.

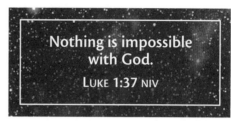

Nothing is impossible with God.
LUKE 1:37 NIV

It was unique.

It was miraculous.

It had never happened before.

And it will never happen again.

In fact, that's how it is with all of God's promises about the first coming of Christ.

> *Christ, by highest heaven adored;*
> *Christ the everlasting Lord!*
> *Late in time behold Him come,*
> *Offspring of the virgin's womb.*
> *Veiled in flesh the Godhead see;*
> *Hail th' incarnate Deity,*
> *Pleased as man with men to dwell,*
> *Jesus, our Emmanuel!*
> *Hark, the herald angels sing,*
> *"Glory to the newborn King."*
> CHARLES WESLEY

*The Lord himself shall give you a
sign; Behold, a virgin shall
conceive, and bear a son, and
shall call his name Immanuel.*

ISAIAH 7:14

*They shall call his name
Emmanuel, which being
interpreted is, God with us.*

MATTHEW 1:23

God with Us

*I*mmanuel. Isn't that a beautiful name? It means "God with us"—three tiny words which, when brought together, have enormous implications.

Back when God created Adam and Eve, He enjoyed intimate fellowship with them. After Adam and Eve ate the forbidden fruit, God was walking in the garden and calling out to them, "Where are you?" (Genesis 3:9 NIV). Evidently the Lord interacted regularly with Adam and Eve, but on this occasion, because the couple had disobeyed God, they attempted to hide from Him. God had also warned that disobedience would bring death, which included spiritual separation from Him. Because of their sin, there was now an impenetrable barrier between the Lord and mankind.

All through the Old Testament, we see this barrier—this insurmountable wall—manifest in different ways. When God drove Adam and Eve out of the Garden of Eden, He assigned cherubim and a flaming sword to prevent any access to the tree of life. When the Lord explained to Moses how to build the Tabernacle (which also determined how the Temple was to be built), He decreed that a heavy veil be placed across the entrance to the Holy of Holies, a clear symbol of the separation between God and people. In the Old Testament nation of Israel, God designated certain individuals as priests, who were to serve as mediators between Him and the Jewish people. The people could not approach God directly; instead, they had to go to a representative of the Lord.

All of this and more affected the perspective the Jewish people had toward God. That they had to offer sacrifices on a regular basis served as a constant reminder of their sinfulness and the separation between themselves and Him. They feared the Lord and saw Him as distant and unapproachable and so holy that they couldn't even pronounce or spell out His full name. And, of course, the Old Testament scriptures made it clear that there was absolutely nothing human beings could do to remove the wall between God and mankind. If ever people were to come back into a personal relationship with God, the Lord Himself would have to do something about the wall.

And do something, He did. Of course, when God does something, He goes all out. He doesn't hold anything back. He is the Author of *every* good and perfect gift; His compassions are new *every* morning. His love for us is infinitely beyond measure. He gave nothing less than His own begotten Son, who took on human flesh and came to earth to dwell among us. Very literally, God was *with* us. Jesus said, "He that hath seen me hath seen the Father" (John 14). The great lengths

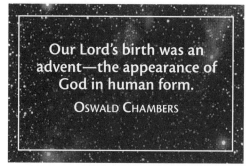

Our Lord's birth was an advent—the appearance of God in human form.

Oswald Chambers

to which God went in order to carry out His plan of redemption show how very much He wanted to draw us back to Him to enjoy intimate fellowship with Him once more. The Lord went so far as to suffer and die an excruciating death for us. That's how much He loved us. That's how much He wanted to restore us.

God with us. God didn't send a messenger; He Himself came to us!

God *with* us. He became a real person like you and me. As a result, He knows our pains and disappointments. And through His death on the cross, He made it possible for us to be redeemed from our sorry state and know true joy and fulfillment.

> In Jesus of Nazareth was seen the mighty God. In the son of the carpenter was seen the Creator of heaven and earth. In the Man of sorrows was seen the Son of the blessed. He who was born at Bethlehem was He whose days are from eternity. He who died was the Prince of life, of whom it is written, "In Him was life, and the life was the light of men."
>
> HORATIUS BONAR

God with *us*. If you have received Jesus Christ as your Savior, He is with you right now—everywhere you go. He has promised He will always stay with you, and He has promised He will never leave you or forsake you.

God with us...three little words so rich with meaning and promise! And the fellowship we experience with God here on earth is just a foretaste of the wonderful relationship we will enjoy with Him in heaven.

For unto us a child is born, unto us a son is given: and the government shall be upon his shoulder: and his name shall be called Wonderful, Counsellor, The mighty God, The everlasting Father, The Prince of Peace.

ISAIAH 9:6

In the beginning was the Word, and the Word was with God, and the Word was God.

JOHN 1:1

The Ultimate Suspense

Come, Thou long expected Jesus...

Charles Wesley

Among the more precious memories my wife, Beverly, and I have are the years when our children were little—and it was Christmastime. The kids couldn't wait to open their presents on Christmas day. They would longingly count the days, eyeing the brightly colored packages under the tree and dying with curiosity over what wonderful treats they might find upon tearing apart the wrapping paper and ribbons.

We can all identify with looking forward to something with great anticipation—opening our presents on Christmas day, the arrival of our wedding day, the birth of our first child or grandchild, or buying a new car or house. But none of these can compare with the tremendous anticipation experienced by God's angels and the Old Testament prophets as they looked forward to the day of Christ's birth.

Can you imagine the overwhelming suspense the prophets felt when they prophesied about the Messiah to come? The apostle Peter said, "The prophets, who spoke of the grace that was to come to you, searched intently and with the greatest care, trying to find out the time and circumstances to which the Spirit of Christ in them was pointing when he predicted the sufferings of Christ and the glories that would follow" (1 Peter 1:10-11 NIV). In the next verse, Peter added that even the angels desired to look into these things. So as the centuries passed and God revealed more and more about the coming Messiah, the suspense became greater and greater. The prophets and angels were probably standing on their tiptoes, trying to see as far as they could into the future in anticipation of Christ's arrival on earth. They knew the tremendous significance of this event—and couldn't wait for it to happen.

When the prophet Isaiah announced that the Christ child would be called "Wonderful, Counsellor, The mighty God, The everlasting Father, The Prince of Peace," that had to raise everyone's anticipation two or three notches. This was no ordinary event, no ordinary birth. This was *God Himself* becoming a man to dwell on earth. This was the day when God's path would directly intersect with man's. When eternity would enter time. When heaven would come to earth. When the perfectly holy One would reach out to the utterly unholy ones.

I'm sure the prophets of old would have given anything to be able to witness that marvelous day with their own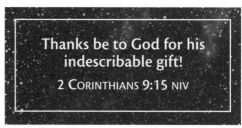

Thanks be to God for his indescribable gift!
2 CORINTHIANS 9:15 NIV

eyes. The suspense must have been unbearable at times. Those of us who are alive today have the privilege of being at the other end of the spectrum. We are able to look back and know all of what happened on the day of Christ's birth. And we also know all about what happened as the divine drama was played out on the stage of human history.

Now that brings up a question: Have you ever noticed how very excited children are before they open their Christmas gifts, but as soon as all the gifts are opened, the mystery and suspense are gone? Their excitement level drops considerably. Certainly they'll play joyfully with their new toys, but in time, even that will wear off. And in just a few months or years, some of those toys may even end up neglected and forgotten in some dark corner of the closet or a drawer.

I fear that, for a lot of us, it's the same way when it comes to God's wonderful promises about Christ's birth, His life on earth, and His death and resurrection. We know the story but we've lost some of our enthusiasm for it. We've sort of left God's promises on a shelf somewhere and haven't taken the time to truly appreciate them.

He has given us his
very great and
precious promises...

2 PETER 1:4 NIV

When was the last time you not only read one of God's promises related to Christ's first coming but actually got down on your knees and thanked Him for it? Have you ever considered what your life would be like if you didn't have any of these promises? Do you talk about these promises with your spouse, your children, your friends? What can you do to make them a more active part of your life?

For the promises connected with Christ's birth, the mystery and suspense are gone. The presents have long been unwrapped. But that shouldn't diminish our appreciation for them at all. Let's cherish them and marvel over them just as the prophets and angels did. Let's thank God for the generosity He has displayed toward us in these promises. Above all, let's thank Him for giving Himself to us. There just isn't any gift greater than that.

There shall come forth a rod out of the stem of Jesse, and a Branch shall grow out of his roots...And in that day there shall be a root of Jesse, which shall stand for an ensign of the people; to it shall the Gentiles seek: and his rest shall be glorious.

ISAIAH 11:1,10

~

The book of the generation of Jesus Christ, the son of David...And Jesse begat David the king...

MATTHEW 1:1,6

No Accidents in
God's Plan

Everything in the future is appointed.
Nothing shall happen to us which
God has not foreseen.

CHARLES SPURGEON

Back in eternity past—before God created the earth and before Adam and Eve made the fatal choice that would bring the world to need a Savior— God knew every single person who would be in the family line that eventually culminated in the birth of Jesus Christ. He knew every married couple, every child, every grandchild, and every subsequent descendant beginning with Adam and Eve and continuing all the way to Joseph and Mary, who became the parents of Jesus. That's why, hundreds of years before Jesus was born, the prophet Isaiah could say the Savior would hail specifically from the family line of Jesse, who was the father of King David.

Consider that there were 1,000 years between the time of Jesse and the birth of Jesus. During those 1,000 years, many marriages and births took place. Humanly speaking, all kinds of things could have happened to mess up the family lineage going from Jesse to the baby Jesus. What if someone didn't marry the "right person" somewhere along the way? What if someone had died prematurely before giving birth to the next person in the line? Considering the many people involved in all the generations from Jesse to Jesus, we cannot help but stand in awe of the fact that God's preordained plan was carried out without a single mishap. As it turned out, Jesus *did* hail from the "root of Jesse." What a wonderful testimony of the fact that we have a totally sovereign God who is in full control of all history and every single human life!

It's also amazing to think that the same God who knew, in advance, every single person in the family line of Jesus also knew all the people who would make up *your* family line. He knew who your parents would be; He knew where you would be born. He knew every single person in your family tree and how their lives would become intertwined in such a way that would ultimately lead to your arrival in the world.

And just as there were no mishaps in the genealogical line of Jesus, there were no mishaps in your family tree. From a human perspective it may appear that mistakes occurred along the way, but from God's perspective, those incidents weren't mistakes. They happened for a purpose, and they aligned with His sovereign plan. While this doesn't mean that if our ancestors made sinful choices God endorsed those choices, it does mean that God's plans are able to continue moving forward in spite of any wrong choices people make.

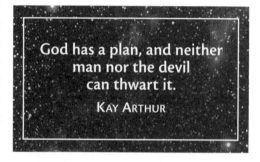

God has a plan, and neither man nor the devil can thwart it.

KAY ARTHUR

Some people picture God as being involved in only the "really important" things here on earth, that He lets all the "small details" just run their course. Even Christians have a hard time fathoming how God could possibly orchestrate the events of every single person's life in order to work out His all-encompassing master plan for the world. But God really does have a handle on everything, and He really does orchestrate every person's life with a specific plan and purpose in mind.

If you want to get a sense for just how important every person is to God, read through the book of Numbers in the Bible. There, you'll find list after list of the names of the tribes and families of the nation of Israel. Many people who read the Bible find these lists rather tedious, but the very fact that God took the time to record all these names shows us that He cared about every person—no matter how seemingly insignificant. In God's eyes, everyone has great significance. And more importantly, every person has a definite place in God's plan for the ages—including you!

In the future, when you wonder about your significance in God's eyes, think about the family lineage of Jesus. God moved all the right people into place to keep that lineage intact, from Adam to Abraham, on down to Jesse and David, and all the way down to Jesus, just as the prophets foretold. In the same way, He made it possible for certain people to come together so that *you* would be on earth at this very moment, for special

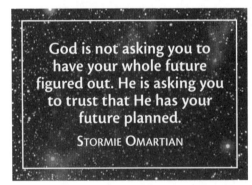

God is not asking you to have your whole future figured out. He is asking you to trust that He has your future planned.

STORMIE OMARTIAN

purposes He has in mind. You might not know what those purposes are yet, but you can be certain God knows what He is doing.

When Israel was a child,
then I loved him,
and called my son out of Egypt.

HOSEA 11:1

∽

When [Joseph] arose, he took
the young child and his mother
by night, and departed into
Egypt: and was there until the
death of Herod: that it might be
fulfilled which was spoken
of the Lord by the prophet,
saying, Out of Egypt have
I called my son.

MATTHEW 2:14-15

A Guarantee That Never Expires

My future is as bright as the promises of God.

ADONIRAM JUDSON

The prophecies about Jesus in the Old Testament are like pieces in a puzzle. The prophecy "I...called my son out of Egypt" is yet one more piece that God revealed to Israel about the promised Messiah. Over time, this puzzle became more and more complete. This future Savior would be born in Bethlehem, born of a virgin, and would be called out of Egypt, among other things. While it's true the words "Israel was a child" refer to God's bringing the people of Israel out of Egypt, Matthew quotes Isaiah's words to affirm that Jesus' return from Egypt was pictured in Israel's earlier exodus from that country.

One of the most important reasons God gave such specific prophecies was to help make it easy for people to identify the true Messiah. The Bible has well over a hundred such prophecies about Christ's first coming, and they all point toward specific truths about the identity of Jesus. They are like signposts lined up all through the Old Testament, pointing toward the one person whom God would send as the Savior of the world.

This also means it would have been impossible for an imposter to claim he was the Savior. It would have been impossible for a yet-to-be-born baby to tell his parents, who lived in Nazareth, to go to Bethlehem for his birth. It would have been impossible for someone to fake the virgin birth. And keep in mind that the reason Joseph and Mary fled to Egypt was because Herod wanted to kill little Jesus. Herod found out about the baby's presence through the wise men, who had traveled a long distance to see him. Who could have orchestrated the wise men's visit as well as Herod's angry response—all in an attempt to claim he was the Messiah?

> The ground of a believer's confidence is not God's smile, but God's promises. It is not his temporary sunshine of his love, but his deep eternal love itself, as it reveals itself in the covenant and in the promises...
>
> CHARLES SPURGEON

There are many more details about Christ's first coming that we haven't touched upon yet—and taken together, they make it overwhelmingly impossible for someone to fake that he is the promised Son of God. The odds are simply too astronomical!

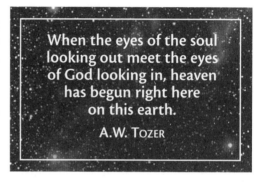

When the eyes of the soul looking out meet the eyes of God looking in, heaven has begun right here on this earth.

A.W. TOZER

Only Jesus fulfilled every single one of these prophecies at every single point.

In a sense, we can also view God's promises to us as signposts that help identify important truths for our lives, too. For example, in Matthew 6:25, God promises to take care of our every physical need. This means we are not to worry about what we will eat or wear. Our heavenly Father wants us to be free of such worry. In James 1:5, we are told, "If any of you lack wisdom, let him ask of God." If we look to God for direction, He will give it to us. God said in Hebrews 13:5, "I will never leave thee, nor forsake thee." Such a promise assures God will never abandon us, and we do not need to fear what others can do to us (see verse 6).

Because every single prophecy about Christ's first coming was fulfilled with perfect precision, we can rest confident that *all* of God's promises to us—His children—will be fulfilled with exactness as well. Now, as we wait for God to fulfill a promise, we probably won't know just how He will make that happen. But we can rest assured that He *will* fulfill His promises—even though we may not know the answers to our questions right away. When God makes a promise, He will keep it. Every promise is backed with a guarantee that never expires. No man can hinder Him from carrying out His work. This assurance should put our hearts to rest about any of the concerns we face today!

The Spirit of the Lord GOD *is upon me; because the* LORD *hath anointed me to preach good tidings unto the meek; he hath sent me to bind up the brokenhearted, to proclaim liberty to the captives, and the opening of the prison to them that are bound; to proclaim the acceptable year of the* LORD, *and the day of vengeance of our God; to comfort all that mourn.*

ISAIAH 61:1-2

He came to Nazareth, where he had been brought up: and...he went into the synagogue on the sabbath day, and stood up for to read...The Spirit of the Lord is upon me, because he hath anointed me to preach the gospel to the poor; he hath sent me to heal the brokenhearted, to preach deliverance to the captives, and recovering of sight to the blind, to set at liberty them that are bruised, to preach the acceptable year of the Lord...And he began to say to them, This day is this scripture fulfilled in your ears.

LUKE 4:16,18-19,21

Who He
Says He Is

*A man who was merely a man and said
the sort of things Jesus said wouldn't be a
great moral teacher...Either this man was
and is the Son of God, or else a madman or
something worse...But don't let us come
up with any patronizing nonsense about
His being a great human teacher. He hasn't
left that open to us. He didn't intend to.*

C.S. Lewis

Is Jesus who He says He is? Is He really the Messiah?

Through the ages, people have given all sorts of wrong answers. In fact, when Jesus asked His own disciples, "Who do people say the Son of Man is?" they answered, "Some say John the Baptist: others say Elijah; and still others, Jeremiah or one of the prophets" (Matthew 16:13-14 NIV).

Even with all the amazing prophetic evidence that points to Jesus as the Messiah, there are many people who deny that Jesus was the one God promised to send. I even know a modern-day Jewish rabbi who has looked at the evidence and reluctantly admits that Jesus was indeed the Messiah—"for the Gentiles"! He believes the "Jewish Messiah" has not yet come.

What is especially intriguing is that even Jesus Himself said He was the fulfillment of Old Testament prophecies. He left no doubt about that. He didn't leave people to guess for themselves about His identity. He proclaimed His Messiahship so clearly it was impossible for people to miss it.

Luke tells us the story in the Bible. In Luke 4, we read that Jesus entered the synagogue in his hometown of Nazareth on the Sabbath day. When he stood up to read, He read from Isaiah 61, where the prophet Isaiah gave a prophecy about

> The Child of the Promise, whose birth and life were foretold centuries before they happened, grew up to be the Messiah the world had long awaited...He came as what the world needed, but many rejected Him because He wasn't what they wanted.
>
> STORMIE OMARTIAN

the future Messiah. Jesus read verses 1 and 2, which describe what the Messiah would do when He came—activities that Jesus was already doing (preaching the gospel, healing the brokenhearted, preaching deliverance to the captives, setting at liberty the oppressed, giving sight to the blind, and so on).

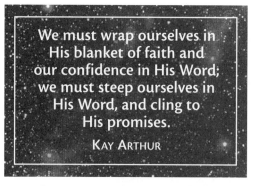

> We must wrap ourselves in His blanket of faith and our confidence in His Word; we must steep ourselves in His Word, and cling to His promises.
>
> KAY ARTHUR

Jesus ended His reading of Isaiah 61 with the words "to preach the acceptable year of the Lord." Then He closed the book of Isaiah and told everyone in the synagogue, "Today this scripture is fulfilled in your hearing" (Luke 4:21 NIV).

Do you know how the people responded? They tried to kill Him! Why? They got the message loud and clear: Jesus was claiming to be the Messiah. They refused to believe that, however. Jesus didn't fit their perceptions of who the Messiah would be. They had expected a glorious and powerful conqueror who would free the Jewish people from the yoke of Roman oppression. Instead, they got a poor teacher who wore a simple robe and had no place to lay His head.

What many people through the ages have not understood is that the Messiah had to suffer first for the sins of the world. That's why, in the prophecy in Isaiah 61 and in Jesus' words in Luke 4, we read about someone who would come to preach the good news to the poor and heal the heartbroken. Jesus was doing exactly what the Messiah was supposed to do. We needed someone to give us spiritual deliverance, not physical. We needed a Savior. Jesus said, "The Son of man is come to seek and to save that which was lost" (Luke 19:10). Later, when He returns, He will come as the King of kings and Lord of lords to set up His kingdom on earth—a kingdom of righteousness, peace, and joy. Our physical deliverance is still future.

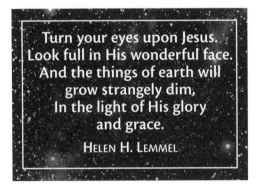

Turn your eyes upon Jesus.
Look full in His wonderful face.
And the things of earth will
grow strangely dim,
In the light of His glory
and grace.

HELEN H. LEMMEL

Who do *you* say Jesus is? Do you truly honor Him as the Messiah, the Savior of the world? Do your prayers and actions toward Him recognize Him as nothing less than God Himself? Your view of Jesus can affect how others around you perceive Him. May everyone around you see clearly, through your words and life, the *real* identity of Jesus.

Moses called for all the elders of Israel, and said unto them, Draw out and take you a lamb according to your families, and kill the passover.

EXODUS 12:21

He was oppressed, and he was afflicted...he is brought as a lamb to the slaughter...

ISAIAH 53:7

Behold the Lamb of God, which taketh away the sin of the world.

JOHN 1:29

The Lamb of God

Behold the Lamb of God!
Worthy is He alone
To sit upon the Throne
Of God above;
One with the Ancient of all days,
One with the Comforter in praise,
All Light and Love.

MATTHEW BRIDGES

What child in Sunday school is not fascinated by the ten plagues in Egypt? What an incredible show of God's awesome power! All ten plagues took place back-to-back and were of monstrous proportions. They would make today's most action-packed thriller movies look feeble by comparison.

Can you list all ten plagues? To refresh our memories: water turns to blood, frogs, lice, flies, death of animals, boils, hail, locusts, three days of darkness, and death of all firstborn.

While all ten plagues were spectacular in and of themselves, there's something different about the last plague, the death of all firstborn, that sets it apart from the others. It was more than just a judgment upon the Egyptians. Within that last plague was a promise from God—a promise that should fill us with thanks and praise every time we think about it.

Keep in mind that during this time, God's people—the people of Israel—were in bondage in Egypt. Moses had repeatedly asked the Pharaoh to let the Israelites go free, but the Pharaoh refused. With each plague, the Pharaoh would momentarily change his mind and tell Moses, "The people can go." But after God stopped each plague, the Pharaoh's heart would harden and he would prohibit the Jewish people from departing.

Before the tenth plague, God gave Moses specific instructions for the people: Take an unblemished lamb, kill it, and place the blood on the doorposts of their homes. On the night of the plague, any home that had blood on the doorposts would be "passed over"—and the firstborn occupants left unharmed. They would not face God's judgment.

This was the plague, of course, that finally set the people free. And from that time onward, all through the Old Testament, the Israelites observed Passover once a year by bringing sacrificial lambs without defect and offering them to the Lord.

Now, let's fast-forward to the day when John the Baptist looks up from the Jordan River and sees Jesus walking toward him and proclaims, "Behold the Lamb of God, which taketh away the

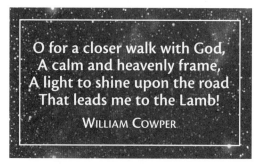

O for a closer walk with God,
A calm and heavenly frame,
A light to shine upon the road
That leads me to the Lamb!

WILLIAM COWPER

sin of the world." Those words were incredibly rich in meaning! How many of the people standing on the banks of the Jordan River that day realized they were looking at the last Passover Lamb—the Lamb who once and for all would free them from spiritual bondage?

Notice that in preparation for the tenth plague, God commanded that the Passover lamb had to be without blemish. God asked the people to give their best to Him—a sacrifice that would be costly. Jesus, too, was a Lamb without blemish. God gave His best to us—a very costly sacrifice. Jesus was without sin and thus was able to become sin for us on the cross.

Notice that the blood of the Passover lamb, when placed upon the doorposts of the people's homes, protected them from God's judgment. Through the shedding of His blood upon the cross, Jesus Christ, the Lamb of God, protects us from God's eternal judgment.

Notice that after the night of that first Passover in Egypt, the people were set free from physical bondage. Jesus Christ, the last Passover Lamb, has set us free from spiritual bondage.

The first Passover was all about redemption—freedom from Egypt. The final Passover—which involved the Lamb of God—was all about redemption, too...the kind that frees us from the fires of hell and promises us eternity in heaven. It's because of Jesus Christ that we can

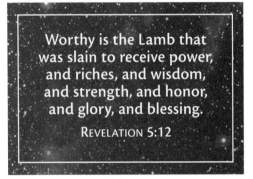

Worthy is the Lamb that was slain to receive power, and riches, and wisdom, and strength, and honor, and glory, and blessing.

REVELATION 5:12

know freedom from sin. From bondage. From guilt. Not just now, but *forever.*

God sent us an extraordinary Lamb, that we might know an extraordinary future.

*He is despised and
rejected of men...*
ISAIAH 53:3

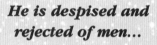

*He came unto his own, and his
own received him not.*
JOHN 1:11

My Heart, Christ's Home

*Let every heart
prepare him room...*

ISAAC WATTS

*I*saiah 53 is one of the most remarkable chapters in all the Old Testament. It predicts, in perfect detail, the future sufferings of the Messiah—700 years *before* Jesus was born! The parallels between Isaiah 53 and the story of Christ's rejection, persecution, and crucifixion are astounding.

You know what else I find amazing? The fact that, after all Jesus had done, He was rejected. Isaiah said this would happen, and the apostle John confirmed that "his own received him not."

Jesus taught as one having authority unlike any person the people had ever heard. His teachings were profound and irrefutable. Yet they rejected Him.

He did countless miracles that were clearly supernatural. He healed the sick and afflicted and fed huge crowds from almost nothing. Yet they rejected Him.

He offered people a way to God that was free of the legalistic bondage imposed by the Jewish spiritual leaders. Yet they rejected Him.

Tragically, not even the 12 disciples did any better. Peter denied Christ not one but three times. Almost all the others fled from the scene when Jesus was crucified. They didn't want to get caught. What did they do to the One who had fed, cared for, and taught them for what had to be the most eye-opening three years of their lives? They abandoned Him.

But before we cluck our tongues in disapproval and say, "I would have stood at Christ's side," let's recall the times we ourselves have rejected or abandoned our Lord...in more subtle ways.

> Salvation is the free gift of God, in Christ Jesus our Lord; and whosoever believeth on him with his whole heart, though his soul be as black as hell itself, shall receive the gift of the Holy Ghost.
>
> GEORGE WHITEFIELD

- Do you hide your Bible or Christian books so your coworkers don't know what you're reading during lunch hour?

- Do you neglect to mention your participation in church-related activities when non-Christian friends ask what you've been up to?

- Do you find yourself secretly hoping no one will ask you questions about your faith and beliefs?

Perhaps you're already thinking of other ways you've quietly disassociated yourself from our Lord. While this is not outright rejection or abandonment, still, we ought to consider how the Lord feels when we shun the privilege of making known His presence in our lives. Wouldn't that make Him feel unwelcome?

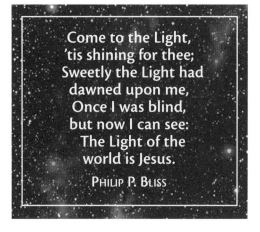

Come to the Light,
'tis shining for thee;
Sweetly the Light had
dawned upon me,
Once I was blind,
but now I can see:
The Light of the
world is Jesus.

PHILIP P. BLISS

Given all that Christ has done for us—especially the fact that He has promised us a life of eternal bliss in heaven—we ought to treat Him as the guest of honor in our lives. Let's make Him feel more welcome. Let's allow the other guests in our lives the opportunity to rub elbows with Him. Let's let our "light so shine before men" that they may "see [our] good works, and glorify [our] Father which is in heaven" (Matthew 5:16).

> For though all things fail, God will never abandon us...
>
> JOHN CALVIN

God promises to never reject or abandon His children. Let's bring joy to His heart and commit to the same in our relationship with Him.

*They pierced my hands
and my feet.*
PSALM 22:16

~

And they crucified him...
MATTHEW 27:35

~

*Then saith [Jesus] to Thomas,
Reach hither thy finger, and
behold my hands; and reach
hither thy hand, and thrust
it into my side: and be not
faithless, but believing.*
JOHN 20:27

No Greater Love

*I know of no truth in the whole Bible that
ought to come home to us with such power
and tenderness as that of the love of God.*

Dwight L. Moody

When King David wrote Psalm 22, little did
he know that he was describing Jesus' crucifixion
some 1,000 years before it happened. More remarkable is the fact that the method of execution, "they
pierced my hands and my feet," *didn't even exist yet.*
It is generally believed that death by crucifixion orig-
inated somewhere in the East and that Alexander the
Great learned of it from the Persians, which would
date its beginnings to approximately the fourth cen-
tury B.C. That's roughly 600 years after David penned
his words.

Once again we have an incredible affirmation
that God knows the future with perfect precision. If
a human had attempted to predict Jesus' death, he
probably would have speculated that Jesus would

die from a stoning. After all, that's how the Jewish people carried out capital punishment in David's day—a method God Himself prescribed in the Bible. Who would have ever guessed that at the time of Jesus, the Roman Empire would rule the known world and would put people to death by nailing them to a cross? Only God could have known.

David could never have imagined just how excruciating death by crucifixion would be. Jesus' crucifixion was carried out by Roman soldiers, and the fact that Rome rarely ever sentenced Roman citizens to such a death should tell us something about how horrible it is. The Romans reserved this kind of punishment only for slaves, serious criminals, assassins, and the like.

John Stevenson, who wrote an eloquent book titled *Christ on the Cross* in 1844, made these comments about the words "they pierced my hands and my feet":

> Of all sanguinary punishments, that of crucifixion is one of the most dreadful...The hands and feet, which are furnished with the most numerous and sensitive organs, are perforated with nails, which must necessarily be of some size to suit their intended purpose. The tearing asunder of the tender fibers of the hands and feet, the lacerating of so many nerves, and

bursting so many blood vessels, must be productive of intense agony. The nerves of the hand and foot are intimately connected, through the arm and leg, with the nerves of the whole body; their laceration therefore must be felt over the entire frame. Witness the melancholy result of even a needle's puncture in even one of the remotest nerves. A spasm is not infrequently produced by it in the muscles of the face, which locks the jaws inseparably. When, therefore the hands and feet of our blessed Lord were transfixed with nails, he must have felt the sharpest pangs shoot through every part of his body. Supported only by his lacerated limbs, and suspended from his pierced hands, our Lord had nearly six hours' torment to endure.

Now, Jesus knew He was going to be crucified...yet He didn't run away from fulfilling God's plan. Can you imagine how very difficult it

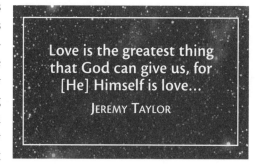

Love is the greatest thing that God can give us, for [He] Himself is love...

JEREMY TAYLOR

must have been for Him to willingly yield to such a death? Jesus didn't go to the cross kicking and screaming. In fact, Hebrews 12:2 says that Jesus "for the *joy* that was set before him endured the cross" (emphasis added).

Jesus looked beyond the pain of the cross and saw that God would be glorified through His sacrificial death. He knew that, as a result, death would be swallowed up in victory, and that for many millions of people—including you and me—this would mean redemption from eternal condemnation and would allow us to enjoy eternal life in heaven with Him.

Jesus faced the cross with joy because He loved us. There is no greater sacrifice that could possibly have been made on our behalf. And there is no greater love that He could have expressed to us. Look to the cross...that's how much He loves you. If you've ever doubted whether He cares, whether He's concerned about your anxieties or troubles, doubt no more. If He went so far as to face crucifixion so that

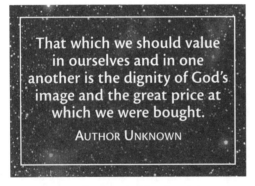

That which we should value in ourselves and in one another is the dignity of God's image and the great price at which we were bought.

AUTHOR UNKNOWN

He could *make* you His child, He will do whatever it takes to *care* for you as His child.

You simply won't find any greater love than that.

*All they that see me laugh me to scorn: they shoot out the lip, they shake the head, saying, He trusted on the L*ORD *that he would deliver him: let him deliver him, seeing he delighted in him.*

PSALM 22:7-8

And the people stood beholding. And the rulers also with them derided him, saying, He saved others; let him save himself, if he be Christ, the chosen of God.

LUKE 23:35

A Promise Made
Is a Promise Kept

He who promised is faithful.
HEBREWS 10:23 NIV

When someone hurts us, what is usually our first reaction? We want to hurt that person back. Sometimes we do so in an overt way, perhaps through harsh words. Other times, we might try to take vengeance in more subtle ways—through malicious gossip about that person or by depriving that person of something good.

Consider the angry little boy who walks away in a huff with his football so that the others can't continue their game. Or the upset little girl who takes her dolls home so the other girls can't continue to play "house." When we don't get our way or feel like others are not playing fair, we'll just quit!

If we're honest with ourselves, we'll admit that this kind of behavior doesn't stop with children. We grown-ups have done quite well at elevating this form of vengeance into an art. We say, "Because you did that to me, I'm *not* going to do that for you."

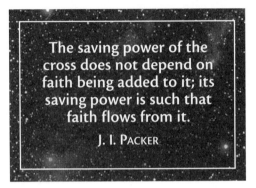

The saving power of the cross does not depend on faith being added to it; its saving power is such that faith flows from it.

J. I. PACKER

How good to know that God isn't like that! He had the perfect opportunity to "quit" when Jesus hung on the cross. Our Lord was surrounded by a hostile crowd. The people jeered at Him. They hurled insults at Him. They laughed, they mocked, they scorned Him. "He says He is the Christ? Let Him save Himself if that's really true!"

How that must have stung God's heart! Can you imagine the enormous restraint God exercised as Jesus hung on the cross? God could have had the earth swallow up all the people or brought down fire from heaven, but He didn't. And did you know that Jesus could have called upon 12 legions of angels at any time to rescue Him (Matthew 26:53)?

Both God and Jesus could have said, "Forget it. This just isn't worth it. Here we are, making the ultimate sacrifice so that you won't have to face eternal punishment for your sin. We're trying to help you, and you could care less. Forget the cross, forget salvation, forget eternal life. You don't deserve it anyway."

But that's not what happened. Jesus stayed on that cross until He died. He endured and paid the horribly high price necessary to redeem us from sin. God didn't say, "Because you rejected me, I'm taking back My promise to give you a Savior."

Even though the disciples had abandoned Jesus and the whole world wanted Him dead, God kept His promise. And He will keep every single one of His promises—no matter what happens. Aren't you grateful He never revokes His promises? Aren't you glad He's not like the little boy who walks off with his football or the little girl who takes her dolls back home?

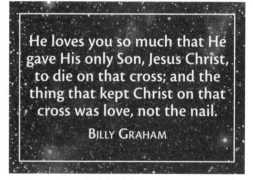

He loves you so much that He gave His only Son, Jesus Christ, to die on that cross; and the thing that kept Christ on that cross was love, not the nail.

BILLY GRAHAM

Won't you take a moment to thank Him...right now?

My God, my God, why hast thou
forsaken me?
PSALM 22:1

~

About the ninth hour Jesus cried
with a loud voice, saying,
Eli, Eli, lama sabachthani?
that is to say,
My God, my God, why hast
thou forsaken me?
MATTHEW 27:46

The Darkest Hour

'Tis mystery all! Th' Immortal dies!
Who can explore His strange design?

CHARLES WESLEY

There are some mysteries so profound that not even the greatest minds in the world could solve them. Specifically, I'm thinking about two mysteries related to the Lord Jesus Christ. They are completely beyond all human comprehension. And I'm glad for that, because it goes to show just how great and awesome a God we have.

The first mystery relates to a prophecy written by King David. About 1,000 years before the crucifixion, he penned the very words Jesus Christ would cry out while upon the cross: "My God, my God, why hast thou forsaken me?"

Those words tell us of something very horrible that happened on the cross—something that had never occurred in all eternity past and will never occur again in the future. When the Son of God hung on the cross and became sin for us, God had to look away and actually forsake His Son. God is so holy that He cannot "look on iniquity" (Habakkuk 1:13). On the cross, Jesus took on Himself the full fury of God's wrath upon sin. He became sin for us and paid the full penalty.

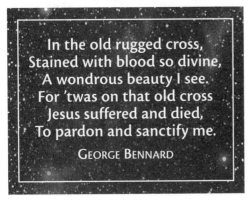

In the old rugged cross,
Stained with blood so divine,
A wondrous beauty I see.
For 'twas on that old cross
Jesus suffered and died,
To pardon and sanctify me.

GEORGE BENNARD

How mind-boggling to think that God the Father—who is one in essence with God the Son and who had enjoyed an intimate fellowship with His Son for all eternity—now had to turn His back on Jesus and pour out all His wrath upon Him!

And, did you know that this is the only time in the entire New Testament Jesus addressed His Father as God? All the other times, Jesus uses the word *Father.* But not here. Can you imagine how utterly painful this must have been for Jesus? Not just the physical pain of the cross, but the fact that He was forsaken by His Father?

That's what Jesus faced for our sake. When I think about that, my heart wells up with tremendous gratitude. What He did for us is a sure sign of how much He loves us.

Then there's the second mystery. As songwriter Charles Wesley put it, "Th' Immortal dies." Because Jesus is God, He is eternal. He had no beginning and has no end. When the prophet Micah predicted Jesus would be born in Bethlehem, he said this child's "goings forth have been from of old, from everlasting." Yet on the cross, He died.

Again, this is beyond our comprehension. Though we cannot understand it, we *can* be grateful. God is infinitely wise and all-knowing, and we as humans are finite and know but a fraction of all there is to know and understand about the spiritual realm.

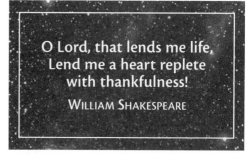

O Lord, that lends me life,
Lend me a heart replete
with thankfulness!

WILLIAM SHAKESPEARE

What I appreciate is that God doesn't demand we understand all of this before we come to Him for salvation. He's got it figured out, and we can rest in that. All He asks is that we believe and trust Him. He did all this so we could be restored into fellowship with Him—so that we could be His children and once again call Him Father. As believers, we will never have to say, as Jesus did, "My God, my God, why hast thou forsaken me?"

We are His children *forever*. Nothing will change that.

He keepeth all his bones: not one of them is broken.

PSALM 34:20

~

Then came the soldiers, and brake the legs of the first, and of the other which was crucified with him. But when they came to Jesus, and saw that he was dead already; they brake not his legs...
For these things were done, that the scripture should be fulfilled, A bone of him shall not be broken.

JOHN 19:32-33,36

No One Can
Defy God's Plan

The Lord is King! Who then shall dare
Resist His will, distrust His care,
Or murmur at His wise decrees,
Or doubt His royal promises?

JOSIAH CONDER

re you familiar with the saying, "God is in the details"? It certainly applies to the prophecies concerning the life of Jesus. In the book of Psalms, God promised that when Jesus died on the cross, not one of His bones would be broken. At first glance, this might seem a rather insignificant detail. But with a closer look, we discover there are a couple reasons this promise is so significant.

First, as we saw earlier, Jesus was "the Lamb of God, which taketh away the sin of the world." He was the final Passover lamb, the sacrifice that set us free from bondage to sin and from God's judgment.

Back in the book of Exodus, when God first initiated the Passover, He said that the Israelites were to choose a lamb "without blemish." Jesus, too, was without blemish.

Another requirement given by God was that none of the bones of a Passover lamb were to be broken. On the cross, none of Jesus' bones were broken. Psalm 34:20 tells us God kept that from happening. So, in every detail, Jesus fulfilled the qualifications of a Passover lamb, which again affirms He is the Messiah that God promised to send.

Here's what else is significant: It was God who determined what would happen to Jesus on the cross, not man. Let me explain.

In ancient Israel, according to God's ceremonial law, the land would become defiled if a dead body was left on a tree overnight. Deuteronomy 21:22-23 NIV says, "If a man guilty of a capital offense is put to death and his body is hung on a tree, you must not leave his body on the tree overnight. Be sure to bury him that same day,

> In the Cross, God descends to bear in His own heart the sins of the world. In Jesus, He atones at unimaginable cost to Himself.
>
> WOODROW A. GEIER

because anyone who is hung on a tree is under God's curse. You must not desecrate the land..."

The Jewish religious leaders who had condemned Jesus to death were anxious for the Roman soldiers to remove the bodies from all three crosses

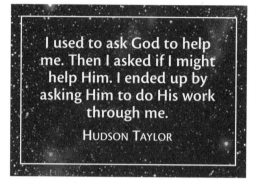

I used to ask God to help me. Then I asked if I might help Him. I ended up by asking Him to do His work through me.

HUDSON TAYLOR

before sundown. So they called upon the soldiers to go ahead and break the legs of all three men so they would die quickly. The only way a person on a cross could stay alive was to push his feet against a small "platform" placed below his feet so he could raise himself upward enough to gasp for air. But if the legs were broken, the victim's body would slump, making it virtually impossible to breathe and thus leading to a quick death.

As the Bible says, the men on both sides of Jesus had their legs broken. This was usually done with a heavy hammer, exacerbating all the more the horror of crucifixion.

But when the soldiers came to Jesus, their experienced eyes could see Jesus was already dead. He had given up his spirit (John 19:30). (This, by the way, lines up with the biblical truth that Jesus would *give up* His life for us and not have it *taken* from Him.) Now, the soldiers could have smashed Jesus' legs just to be cruel. They could have said, "Let's do this just to make sure." No, God overruled any inclination they might have had on their part. God promised none of Jesus' bones would be broken, and He prevented that from happening at the cross.

So, here we see God in full control of human events. He held back the hands of the Roman soldiers—soldiers who were *not* believers. In fact, every detail of the crucifixion happened exactly the way God promised it would, even though Jesus' trial and death were carried out by religious leaders and Roman military men who had nothing to do with God. Every one of these people was, without knowing it, carrying out God's own plan to perfection. Unwittingly, they were cooperating with God.

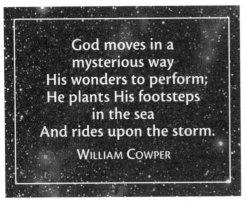

God moves in a
mysterious way
His wonders to perform;
He plants His footsteps
in the sea
And rides upon the storm.

WILLIAM COWPER

Do you know what that means for you and me today? No unbeliever today can do anything against us unless, for some reason or other, God allows it. No matter what happens to us, God is in full control. No one can take matters out of God's hands—ever.

God's plans will always move forward, uninterrupted. And that includes His plans for you and me. When things go wrong, we can know He is still in charge. He's still calling the shots. Of that, we can be absolutely certain.

He was pierced for our transgressions, be was crushed for our iniquities...and by his wounds we are healed.

ISAIAH 53:5 NIV

~

He himself bore our sins in his body on the tree...by his wounds you have been healed.

1 PETER 2:24 NIV

The Empty Cross

*God forbid that I should glory, save in
the cross of our Lord Jesus Christ.*

GALATIANS 6:14

Several years ago I (Tim) wrote a book entitled *The Power of the Cross*, showing the transforming power of the Holy Spirit in the lives of those who bend their knees before the cross and by faith receive the finished work of Christ for their sins. In preparation for the writing I interviewed more than 200 people from all walks of life who were wearing a cross. Actually, I found it is the most popular piece of jewelry in our day. I asked each person two simple questions: 1) "Why do you wear that cross?" and 2) "What does it mean to you?"

The answers I received were amazing. No one took offense, and everyone had a reason for wearing it. Some cross wearers had no idea what it meant and said so. Some wore it as "just a piece of jewelry." One man said, "My grandmother gave it to me for Christmas, and since I am on my way to visit her, I thought I had better wear it."

Many gave very meaningful responses—for example, the young schoolteacher who held her cross on a gold chain in her hand and said with tears, "It means everything to me—Jesus, who hung on that cross for my sins, died and rose again on the third day. He heard my cry for forgiveness and saved me.

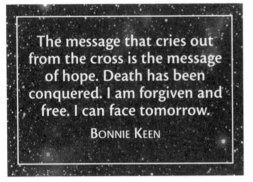

The message that cries out from the cross is the message of hope. Death has been conquered. I am forgiven and free. I can face tomorrow.

BONNIE KEEN

It is through Him that this cross represents I have the assurance I will go to heaven someday."

I couldn't have said it better! For that is what the cross means to me—everything.

On our seventh wedding anniversary my wife Beverly gave me a black onyx ring with a gold cross on it. I have worn it now for over 40 years as a visible symbol that the most important event of my life was when I asked the resurrected Christ of that cross to forgive my sin and save me. Today I credit the thousands of blessings in my life to Him for not only saving me but also for guiding my life.

And that is the most important reason I prefer an empty cross to a crucifix. I never fault those who wear a crucifix, for they obviously are sincere and want to be reminded of the One who died for them. While that is admirable, if Christ had not risen from the dead, we would be, as Paul said, "yet in [our] sins." The empty cross reminds us not only of Jesus' crucifixion, but it also is a visual reminder that He rose triumphant over death and the tomb and is ready and available to guide us in the many decisions we must make in our daily lives.

Jesus lives! We do not worship a dead Savior, but one who is alive and at the right hand of God, making intercession for us. One who not only saved us, but who is willing to guide us as we make the decisions of life.

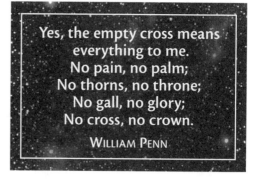

Yes, the empty cross means everything to me.
No pain, no palm;
No thorns, no throne;
No gall, no glory;
No cross, no crown.

WILLIAM PENN

Jonah was inside the fish three days and three nights.

JONAH 1:17 NIV

A wicked and adulterous generation asks for a miraculous sign! But none will be given it except the sign of the prophet Jonah. For as Jonah was three days and three nights in the belly of a huge fish, so the Son of Man will be three days and three nights in the heart of the earth.

MATTHEW 12:39-40 NIV

No Ordinary
Three-Day Weekend

Before Christ's resurrection,
it was twilight; it is sunrise now.

AUGUSTUS H. STRONG

C an you imagine the disciples' great disappointment after Jesus was buried?

Just a week earlier, Jesus had ridden into
Jerusalem on the colt of a donkey, surrounded by an
enthusiastic throng of people praising Him and
shouting, "Hosanna to the son of David! Blessed is
He that cometh in the name of the Lord! Hosanna in
the highest!" That Jesus was on the colt of a donkey
followed the tradition of Israeli kings entering into
the city in the same way. And that the crowd called
Jesus "the son of David" shows they recognized His
royal status.

That must have gotten the disciples excited. Was
this a sign that Jesus would soon be crowned as

king? Was He finally going to usher in this kingdom He had taught about over the last three years? Would they now become His prestigious officials and no longer be poor servants living a somewhat nomadic lifestyle?

In a private conversation the disciples had with Jesus in Matthew chapter 24, Jesus tells them that one day, the Temple in Jerusalem would be destroyed. That was the exact opposite of what the disciples had expected! Confused and alarmed, they asked Jesus, "What shall be the sign of thy coming, and of the end of the world?" They thought Jesus was about to set up His kingdom, and they wanted to know if it would happen soon.

But now, one week later, the same crowds that had cheered Jesus turned against Him, the crown of gold the disciples had anticipated turned out to be a crown of thorns, and instead of a seat upon a throne, Jesus was nailed to a cross. The one whom the disciples had loved and followed for three years was now dead and buried. Their whole world had completely collapsed; their hopes and anticipation had turned into fear and trepidation.

What were they to do now?

We who have the benefit of hindsight know that the story would have a good ending. But the disciples thought it was all over. Their beloved Master was gone, and the kingdom they had expected would never come. Notice that on Sunday morning when Mary Magdalene ran to the disciples to tell them Jesus had risen, they *refused* to believe her (Mark 16:11 NASB)! Even though Jesus had told the disciples about His death and resurrection many times, they couldn't believe the report about the empty tomb.

During His ministry, Jesus had taught, "For as Jonah was three days and three nights in the belly of a huge fish, so the Son of Man will be three days and three nights in the heart of the earth" (Matthew 12:39-40 NIV). And just days before the crucifixion, while Jesus and the disciples were making their way to Jerusalem, He told them, "Behold, we go up to Jerusalem; and the Son of man shall be delivered unto the chief priests, and unto the scribes; and they shall condemn him to death, and shall deliver him to the Gentiles: and they shall mock him, and shall scourge him, and shall spit upon him, and shall kill him: *and the third day he shall rise again*"

> You know with all your heart and soul that not one of all the good promises the LORD your God gave you has failed. Every promise has been fulfilled.
>
> JOSHUA 23:14 NIV

(Mark 10:33-34, emphasis added). In fact, Jesus mentioned His resurrection several times to the Twelve, but apparently this truth didn't sink into their minds.

I rejoice in your promise like one who finds great spoil.

PSALM 119:162

So while Jesus was in the grave, instead of waiting in confident hope, the men cowered away in their fears and doubts.

How many times have we done that, too? How many times have we read Jesus' promises in the Bible, only to forget them? Sometimes our problem is that we don't read the Bible enough, so we don't even know what He has promised us. Other times, we have selective hearing—we accept only those promises that we think can be fulfilled and doubt the others. Or, we read His promises but don't even pay attention to them—much like the disciples apparently hadn't paid attention.

When we don't know God's promises, we'll find ourselves filled with doubt and uncertainty about life and the future—just as the disciples were. It's only when we pay attention and trust God to fulfill His promises that we can have an unshakeable confidence and hope at all times, no matter what happens. If you want that to be true about your life, cultivate the habit of remembering God's promises… starting today!

Thou wilt not leave my soul in hell; neither wilt thou suffer thine Holy One to see corruption.

PSALM 16:10

He seeing this before spake of the resurrection of Christ, that his soul was not left in hell, neither his flesh did see corruption. This Jesus hath God raised up, whereof we all are witnesses.

ACTS 2:31-32

The Wonder of the Resurrection

The resurrection morning was only the beginning of a great, grand and vast outreach that has never ended and will not end until our Lord Jesus Christ comes back again.

A.W. TOZER

Without the resurrection, Christianity would be just another world religion. Our God would be no more powerful than any other god. In fact, if God hadn't raised Jesus from the dead, it would have proven Christianity to be a fraud.

That's why the apostle Paul based all his teaching on the fact of the resurrection. He knew it was the one event that proved the truthfulness of the Bible and the trustworthiness of God Himself. He wrote,

If Christ be not risen, then is our preaching vain, and your faith is also vain. Yea, and we are found false witnesses of God; because we have testified of God that he raised up Christ (1 Corinthians 15:14-15).

So, you can see why all of Christianity is totally dependent on the resurrection. If we know the resurrection really happened, then we can trust all the rest of the Bible. We can know our faith is not in vain. In fact, the resurrection is the greatest of all signs that confirms Jesus' deity and God's power. No one else in all history has ever risen from the dead or raised someone else up from death. Jesus alone raised people from the dead during His ministry on earth, and only Jesus had the power to conquer death.

Now, there are some people who say the resurrection never happened. They say that Jesus rose spiritually and not physically, or they try to deny the resurrection altogether. But the evidence for this event is too overwhelming. The apostles themselves were eyewitnesses who recorded what they saw, and they were explicit that Jesus appeared to them in *bodily* form. In fact, Jesus affirmed His bodily resurrection when He said, "Behold my hands and my feet, that it is I myself: handle me, and see; for

a spirit hath not flesh and bones, as ye see me have"
(Luke 24:39).

The burden of proof is upon the skeptics who
dismiss the resurrection. None of their explanations
adequately deals
with the fact that
one man—Jesus
Christ—has had
such an over-
whelmingly
powerful impact
on the world that
continues
through today,
transforming
hundreds of mil-
lions of lives all
over the globe.
No one else has
come even close

> If the premises of the
> Christian view are correct as
> to Christ's claim to be the
> Son of God, and as to the
> connection of sin with
> death, it was impossible that
> He, the Holy One, should be
> holden of death. The Prince
> of Life must overcome death.
> His resurrection is the
> pledge that death shall yet
> be swallowed up in victory.
>
> DAVID ORR

to having a similar impact—not even the great military
conquerors of the past who commanded armies num-
bering hundreds of thousands of soldiers. Jesus took
the world by storm with just a dozen men in simple
robes and sandals.

There are several reasons for believing the resurrection. Let's look at just three of them here:

1. *The empty tomb*—Jesus' tomb is the only one in the world that's famous for what it does *not* contain. Consider that both Jesus' friends and enemies verified that the tomb was empty. The enemies didn't want the body gone, and the Roman soldiers who were guarding the tomb knew they would be put to death if the body were missing. They had a strongly vested interest in keeping the body in that grave. And the disciples, as we saw earlier, didn't believe the tomb was empty at first.

2. *The lack of a body*—If the Jewish religious leaders responsible for Jesus' crucifixion had wanted to disprove the resurrection, all they needed to do was produce Jesus' dead body. But they couldn't. That's why, when the apostles preached salvation in the resurrected Jesus Christ, thousands of Jewish people became Christians. The people who were living in Jerusalem at the time knew the resurrection story was fully credible. If the account hadn't been credible, there's no way Christianity could have continued for more than a few days. It would have immediately been revealed as a hoax. But that didn't happen.

3. *The changed lives of the eyewitnesses*—Some skeptics say the disciples didn't actually see the resurrected Christ but were deluded or experiencing hallucinations. That's unlikely, however, because at first, the men themselves doubted that Jesus had risen. They were slow to believe, wanting to see the evidence for themselves. And once they were convinced, they were radically

> For if we believe that Jesus died and rose again, even so them also which sleep in Jesus will God bring with him...Wherefore comfort one another with these words.
>
> 1 THESSALONIANS 4:14,18

transformed—to the point of becoming zealous witnesses of the Gospel message, even willing to die for their beliefs. The early Christians who followed in the footsteps of the apostles were persecuted horribly. They were imprisoned, thrown to the lions, beaten, boiled in oil, and burned. That they were willing to die for their faith demonstrates the depth of their conviction that Jesus had indeed risen from the dead.

My friend, God promised Jesus would rise from the dead, and that's exactly what happened. The evidence for the resurrection is overwhelming. And do you know what that means to us? That death itself has been conquered, and that we have no reason to fear death. For believers, death is simply the entryway to eternal life. As Charles Spurgeon put it, "Jesus has transformed death from a dreary cavern into a passage leading to glory." And as another person wrote, "Death for the Christian is an honorable discharge from the battles of life."

> With the resurrection the uncertainty ends. It is not only that the immediate darkness passes, but the troublesome mists are lifted as well, and the Master emerges as the clearly manifested Son of God. "Arise, shine, for thy light is come, and the glory of the Lord is risen upon thee!"
>
> DR. J. H. JOWETT

Because the Lord Jesus Christ rose from the dead, we will rise, too, if we have trusted Him as our Savior. We have no reason to fear death because of what comes afterward. We too, will know the power of the resurrection.

Lives again our glorious King,
Alleluia
Where, O Death, is now thy sting?
Alleluia
Dying once He all doth save,
Alleluia
Where thy victory, O Grave?
Alleluia

Love's redeeming work is done,
Alleluia
Fought the fight, the battle won,
Alleluia
Death in vain forbids Him rise,
Alleluia
Christ hath opened Paradise,
Alleluia

CHARLES WESLEY

Know therefore that the LORD thy God, he is God, the faithful God...

DEUTERONOMY 7:9

~

Faithful is he that calleth you, who also will do it.

1 THESSALONIANS 5:24

Trusting in God's Faithfulness

If God's goodness to us be like the morning light, which shines more and more to the perfect day, let not ours to him be like the morning cloud and the early dew that pass away.

MATTHEW HENRY

ll through this book, we have seen God's faithfulness marvelously on display in the prophecies about Christ's first coming. God promised Jesus would be born of a virgin in the town of Bethlehem. He promised His Son would come forth from Egypt, and that He would come as a Savior. He predicted with astounding accuracy the details of Jesus' betrayal and crucifixion. Most important of all, He said the Messiah would rise from the dead, making it possible for us to enjoy eternal life in God's presence. Every single one of these promises was fulfilled, as well as

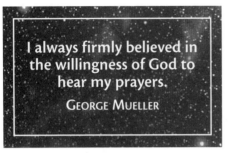

I always firmly believed in the willingness of God to hear my prayers.

GEORGE MUELLER

more than 100 others related to Christ's first coming.

Now, that's just a portion of all the promises that appear in the Bible. You and I have many other great and precious promises God has given us. Let's look at a few of them:

1. *God will provide for our every need*—Jesus said, "I tell you, do not worry about your life, what you will eat or drink; or about your body, what you will wear. Is not life more important than food, and the body more important than clothes?... So do not worry, saying, 'What shall we eat?' or 'What shall we drink?' or 'What shall we wear?' For the pagans run after all these things, and your heavenly Father knows that you need them" (Matthew 6:25,31-32 NIV).

2. *God will give us wisdom when we need it*— The apostle James wrote, "If any of you lack wisdom, let him ask of God...and it shall be given him" (James 1:5).

3. *God will never give us more than we can bear*—"There hath no temptation taken you but such as is common to man: but God is faithful, who will not suffer you to be tempted above that ye are able; but will with the temptation also make a way to escape, that ye may be able to bear it" (1 Corinthians 10:13).

4. *God is always present at our side*—"Though I walk through the valley of the shadow of death, I will fear no evil: for thou art with me..." (Psalm 23:4).

5. *Nothing can separate us from God's love*— "Who shall separate us from the love of Christ? Shall tribulation, or distress, or persecution, or famine, or nakedness, or peril, or sword? ...For I am persuaded, that neither death, nor life, nor angels, nor principalities, nor powers, nor things present, nor things to come, nor height, nor depth, nor any other creature, shall be able to separate us from the love of God, which is in Christ Jesus our Lord" (Romans 8:35,38-39).

6. *He has given us a guide for all of life*—"When he, the Spirit of truth, comes, he will guide you into all truth" (John 16:13 NIV).

7. *He will take us to heaven someday*—"In my Father's house are many mansions: if it were not so, I would have told you. I go to prepare a place for you. And if I go and prepare a place for you, I will come again, and receive you unto myself; that where I am, there ye may be also" (John 14:2-3).

Did you read those promises carefully? If you are a Christian, every single one of them applies to *you!* There is nothing small or insignificant about these promises. They are magnificent in every way, and they speak of just how wonderful a God we have. And those promises are just a fraction of the many more that are in the Bible!

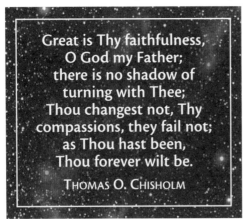

Great is Thy faithfulness,
O God my Father;
there is no shadow of
turning with Thee;
Thou changest not, Thy
compassions, they fail not;
as Thou hast been,
Thou forever wilt be.

THOMAS O. CHISHOLM

In the future, whenever you come across a promise in Scripture, you might want to mark it or write it on an index card so you can memorize it. God's promises can lift us up in the times when we're struggling with doubts or discouragement. His assurances are intended to get us to look to Him for help rather than to our own inadequate selves. And there's no better way to restore our hope and confidence than to reflect on His promises and remind ourselves that God *always has* and *always will* keep His promises.

*Do not forget this one thing,
that with the Lord one day is as
a thousand years, and a
thousand years as one day. The
Lord is not slack concerning
His promise, as some count
slackness, but is longsuffering
toward us, not willing that any
should perish but that all
should come to repentance.
But the day of the Lord will
come as a thief in the
night...We, according to His
promise, look for new heavens
and a new earth in which
righteousness dwells.*

2 PETER 3:8-10,13 NKJV

The Lord Keeps
His Promises

*The greatness of the Promiser enhances
the greatness of the promises.*

A. R. FAUSSET

Everyone has experienced the disappointment of broken promises. As a pastor, I (Tim) have counseled and suffered with people who were living with the consequences of broken promises. I have also encountered the promise-breakers. I remember a 62-year-old man who abandoned his needy, sick wife for a younger woman. When questioned about the integrity of his wedding promise, he snapped his fingers indifferently and said, "Promises are like pie crusts, made to be broken."

Not so with God! There are no promises God has not kept. He promised through the ancient Hebrew prophets that Jesus would come. He kept that promise right on time. When Jesus came He also promised to come again. He said He would later return to the earth and set up His thousand-year kingdom. You may trust that this promise also will be kept on time.

Peter tried to explain this on a level that we humans could understand. God's promise to return was made 2000 years ago, but since God regards "a thousand years as one day" this pledge is but as a two-day-old promise. Human promises tarnish with age. Not God's! His Word is forever settled in heaven.

In this passage, Peter also tells us why Christ has so long delayed His coming. He is "not willing that any should perish but that all should come to repentance." Let every believer trumpet this from the housetops: God wants no one to be lost.

Somehow a false characterization of God has been spread by the deceiver. He has sponsored the stern notion that God is an angry taskmaster who delights in throwing people into hell. Nothing could be further from the truth! God loves humanity so much that He gave His Son to save us. He stands at the edge of hell, weeping when anyone is lost. Surely this must prove how much God loves humankind.

Since God is "not slack concerning His promise," we know beyond a shadow of a doubt that Jesus is coming again. Our number one task is to be ready when He comes. The only way we can be sure of our preparedness is to personally receive His Son, Jesus, as our Lord. Have you prepared yourself and drawn near to the Savior?

From the beginning of time, when Adam and Eve chose to disobey God, sin entered into the human race. Every person is born a sinner. Sin created a chasm between God and man that could not be bridged until His divine and holy Son Jesus identified with the human race by becoming one of us through the vir-gin birth. This made it possible for a holy God to not only iden-tify with us but also become the sacrifice for our sins. Since the cross, it has been possible for man to come back to God by stepping

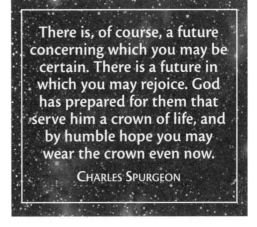

> There is, of course, a future concerning which you may be certain. There is a future in which you may rejoice. God has prepared for them that serve him a crown of life, and by humble hope you may wear the crown even now.
>
> CHARLES SPURGEON

out on faith and receiving Christ personally. Those who accept Him will enter heaven, and those who don't will die in their sins and be judged.

Have you personally trusted Jesus to forgive your sin and provide you with eternal life? If you haven't, we invite you to express your trust in Christ with the following prayer:

> *"Dear God, thank You for sending Your Son Jesus to die on the cross for my sins. I confess I am a sinner, and I ask You for Your forgiveness. Today I want to trust Jesus as my Lord and Savior. I give my life and future to You. In Jesus' name I pray, Amen."*

If you have already received Christ, you have a wonderful future ahead of you! God's promises about heaven are so great as to be beyond our imagination. And because He is all-powerful, we know that He will make every single one of those promises come to pass.

Our hope is that you've been greatly encouraged as you've learned more about God's promises in this book—that you've come to see more of God's greatness, His faithfulness, and His love for you.

Your promises have been thoroughly tested, and your servant loves them.

PSALM 119:140 NIV

Hymn writer Isaac Watts captured well the truth of God's never-ending faithfulness to us and the surety of our hope when he wrote these words:

O God our Help in ages past,
  our Hope for years to come,
Our Shelter from the stormy blast,
  and our eternal Home!

Under the shadow of Thy throne
  still may we dwell secure;
Sufficient is Thine arm alone,
  and our defense is sure.

Before the hills in order stood,
  or earth received her frame,
From everlasting Thou art God,
  to endless years the same.

O God our Help in ages past,
  our Hope for years to come,
Be Thou our Guide while life shall last,
  and our eternal Home!

Beloved, now are we the sons of God, and it doth not yet appear what we shall be: but we know that, when he shall appear, we shall be like him; for we shall see him as he is. And every man that hath this hope in him purifieth himself, even as he is pure.

1 JOHN 3:2-3

The Hope of
Every Believer

*The certainty of the second coming of Christ should
touch and tincture every part of our daily behavior.*

JOHN BLANCHARD

ll through this book we have looked at
prophecies related to the first coming of Jesus Christ.
Jerry and I now want to close with a look to the
future at the second coming—a truly spectacular
event that can happen anytime soon!

The return of our Lord Jesus Christ is the hope of
the Christian. We have already seen that only God
can guarantee our future, and only He can predict it.
Many others have tried, but their prophecies have
never come to pass.

Our God is different. He has an unbroken chain
of hundreds of accurately fulfilled prophecies.
Remember Nebuchadnezzar's dream? Daniel interpreted it in such a way as to explain to the despot

that four world empires would come and remain until the last days (Daniel 2:27-45). So far, history has vindicated Daniel. Much of what he prophesied has come to pass, right on schedule. We have already seen the miracle of the Jews returning to Israel. The reason many other prophecies have not been fulfilled is that they are still in the future. That is what prophecy is: history written ahead of time! Anyone can make "iffy" predictions, but only God can write history in advance and have it come to pass.

> Christian hope far surpasses this idea of wishing, and instead it is a longing for what will certainly happen. In other words, rather than a wish, hope is a promise, the promise of eternal life; and it is Christ that is our hope.
>
> PETER LYNCH

Jerry and I want Christians everywhere to become excited about Jesus' second coming. This isn't a matter of guesstimate or supposition; it is a certified fact of the future. We can't guarantee Jesus will come in our lifetime, although we expect Him to. But we can guarantee He will come again, for He always does all He has promised.

When He does come, what will we be like? This is one of the most common questions we are asked at prophecy conferences. Jerry and I always answer confidently that we will be like Jesus, "for we shall see him as he is" (1 John 3:2). This gives us hope for the future.

Such hope is, as the apostle Paul says, a confident expectation of life in the afterlife with our Lord (2 Corinthians 5:6). It is not a shaky hope like when we hope a friend will keep his word. It is God's hope we are considering. It is our eternal hope, as certain as His Word and as confident as His promise.

Sadly, not everyone shares this hope. Those who reject Christ have no hope. Christ alone can guarantee our hope. Friend, do you have this hope? Trust its author! You have nothing to lose and everything to gain. Someone has wisely said, "For a Christian, this present life is as bad as it will ever get. For the unbeliever, it's as good as it will ever get." The confident expectation of Christ's second coming makes the difference.

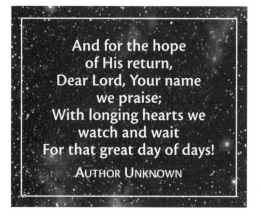

And for the hope
of His return,
Dear Lord, Your name
we praise;
With longing hearts we
watch and wait
For that great day of days!

AUTHOR UNKNOWN

What a blessed gift, this wonderful hope.

> I wait for the Lord, my
> soul doth wait, and in
> his word do I hope.
>
> PSALM 130:5

Other Good Reading

Tim LaHaye and Jerry Jenkins

Are We Living in the End Times? The biblical foundation for the *LEFT BEHIND® SERIES* of novels (Tyndale House Publishers).

Perhaps Today: Living in the Light of Christ's Return. A ninety-day devotional treatment of Second Coming Scriptures that is both instructive and inspirational (Tyndale House Publishers).

THE LEFT BEHIND® SERIES. Eleven exciting novels based on the prophetic Scriptures (Tyndale House Publishers).

The Promise of Heaven. An inspiring collection of Scriptures, classic quotes, and personal prayers and writings in a beautifully decorated volume (Harvest House Publishers).

Tim LaHaye and Thomas Ice

Charting the End Times. This visual resource of charts and well-written explanatory text provides a fascinating picture of the times ahead (Harvest House Publishers).

Charting the End Times Prophecy Study Guide. An interactive study about the Rapture, the Tribulation, the return of Christ, the judgment, the Millennial kingdom, heaven, and more (Harvest House Publishers).

For more information on these and other great books, visit

www.leftbehind.com
www.tyndale.com
www.harvesthousepublishers.com